The Daec

MANDY PANNETT

SPM Publications
London

SPM Publications
www.spmpublications.com
publisher@spmpublications.com

First published in the United Kingdom by SPM Publications – an imprint of Sentinel Writing & Publishing Company in March 2021.

ISBN: 978-1-9162263-5-7

Sentinel Writing & Publishing Company is a trading style of SPM Publications Ltd.

Dedication

To Médecins Sans Frontières for their work with displaced persons around the world.

Books by Mandy Pannett

Bee Purple	Oversteps Books 2002
Frost Hollow	Oversteps Books 2006
Allotments in the Orbital	Searle Publishing 2009
All the Invisibles	SPM Publications 2012
Jongleur in the Courtyard	Indigo Dreams Publishing 2015
Ladders of Glass	Integral Contemporary Literature Press 2017 (English & Romanian texts)
The Onion Stone	(Novella) Pewter Rose Press 2011
The Wulf Enigma	(Novella) Circaidy Gregory Press 2019

NOTES ON THE DAEDALUS FILES

It's possible that Daedalus was a person who later became part of a myth. He was known for his skill as an architect, craftsman, inventor and sculptor of many things including statues that moved and seemed lifelike. When King Minos was cursed by the gods and his wife Pasiphae tricked into lusting after a bull, Daedalus fashioned a realistic wooden cow that she could lie inside and so mate with the bull. The product of this union was the Minotaur, a monstrous creature, half-human, half-animal.

Daedalus also designed a massive labyrinth for the minotaur to be kept in. Young men and women were brought over from Athens to Crete in a ship with a black sail to be sacrificed to the beast. Eventually, Theseus, with the help of thread given to him by the king's daughter Ariadne, made his way through the labyrinth and killed the Minotaur. Theseus escaped with Ariadne but later seems to have abandoned her on the island of Naxos.

Daedalus and his son Icarus were imprisoned in a tower by the king but Daedalus designed wings made from feathers so they could escape. Both managed to fly for a considerable distance but Icarus went too close to the sun, his wings melted and he fell, drowning in the sea.

So much for the story. I first became interested – later obsessed – by Daedalus, a few years ago when we were staying with our friends Lynn and JB on the beautiful Greek island of Tilos. Somehow we started talking about Icarus and the Icarian Sea named after him and maybe it was because we were so close to the blue, shimmering water that the sad tale began to feel real. While we were there a boatload of refugees from Syria tried to land on the rocks but was intercepted and scores of men, women and children were later brought down to the harbour to wait for a ship that would take them to a holding centre in Athens. It was tragic to see and to think about. Daedalus and Icarus were trying to escape, these refugees had wanted to escape. The two things connected in my imagination and that same day I began the poem that became 'Memo'.

Over the years I have explored the myth of Daedalus, discovering threads of loss, betrayal and abandonment, the nature of monstrosity, the down-treading of women, the desire for flight. A myth is more than an ancient, half-forgotten tale; themes in the story of Daedalus feel as relevant today as they ever were.

Mandy Pannett

ACKNOWLEDGEMENTS

Thanks to the editors of Envoi, International Times and The High Window who have published versions of some of these poems.

Special thanks for this pamphlet to Nnorom Azuonye at SPM Publications. Also, to Caroline Maldonado, a perfect friend and writing critic. Thanks also to Val Bridge, Judith Cair, Gill McEvoy and Jocelyn Simms for their generous endorsements and also, of course, to my own writing group; the Green Room Poets and to all the members of the Arun, Slipstream and River Poet groups whose encouragement and interest over the years has been invaluable. Last, but never least, thanks to my lovely family for all their support.

Contents

THE DAEDALUS FILES

He leaves the thickness of the darker ground
where words dry up like a chick's
                    thin bones

            and he feels his own bones lifting as he slips out
of gravity and soars
                    wherever the winds allow

The Black Sail 1

Leaving is a song of sadness, a keening
in the wetlands like cries of geese and gulls –
but there's no agony in this word, no skull
in the catacombs white and screaming,
no heart ripped out, no untimely weaning
when daughters are raped, enslaved, no cull
of a woman's sons. The child's footfall
washes away. And this is what leaving means.

As it must have meant, in myth or in fact
to the mothers of Athens whose children
vanished, sacrificed to a monstrous cause
just because, oh just because of an act
of folly, secret itineraries and hidden
deceits. Pointless, the dying because.

Strange Things, Maker

Twists inside your soul
are well concealed.

You perfect an outward
show, that of a rude

mechanical, an extraordinary maker
of strange things – fantastic

to men of Rhodes who watch, amazed,
as statues yawn, step

off platforms, flexing necks,
sluggards too long in their sloth

or elderly couch-potatoes
stiff from over-slump.

Daedalus, it is recorded
that one word from you and these statues

turned into robots in Grecian cloth
with eyeballs that altered from marble

to jelly, from blank
to the blue of the sea.

And these your creations
then breathed in gulps of waterside air and sang

in rusty, clockwork tones
at the rise and set of the sun.

Are you proud of them
your automata

or is it all too easy for you,
transitory and insignificant?

Question: Sweetness and the Spark

At what point, Daedalus, does a toxin
get created from scratch, a cure for cancer
or ebola lost in the push for a noxious
virus, bombs in the desert financed
by those who declare that the end must
always justify the means and only mugs
count the bodies, count the devilish cost?
Was the technical sweetness a drug?
You should have noticed the birdless trees,
the unsplashing fish rivers, the cold bees.

Or were you in love with the spark, an incident
in prehistory's gloom, a sudden cry of pain
when two stones were accidentally
struck together and so made a flame.
Did it burn for a while, that first hot brand,
then sink into ash with the skill quite lost
for millennia of winds until, at random,
it occurred again, fire – and the later dust
from the witch on the pyre, the pilot
in the burning cage. Tell me, was it worth it?

Answer: If it Wasn't for Me

Enough to untangle my own labyrinth.
    I am not accountable
                for tinkering fingers

since invention is not concerned with the gods
    neither do a craftsman's plans share frontiers
                with any heaven or hell.

What begins in simplicity
    may be mangled into terror –
                but in the meantime

discovery is addictive; a dopamine kick.
    If I offered you a pot and wooden spoon
                you would cook

soup and so feed your belly –
    but I can hear tunes in the bark of a tree
                notice a tool

sharp and precise
    in the bones of a flatfish stripped by gulls
                thin to its spine on the sand.

You say my devices lead us to death. I say
    if it wasn't for me you would not possess
                this, this, this ...

Light and the Darker Half

It's winter, season
of the darker half,
sky as dull as thin
green tea. Shadows
may be a huddle
of crows.

The wood is a marquee
of strangeness:
there are faces behind
the leaves as a blackbird
in full-throated song
halts, cut-off, choked.

This is the realm
of the Queen of Death
whose harbingers, beaked
like birds, crush
every last bud
of inspiration.

The Craftsman Tells of a Way to Make Fear

From the beginning
                                        there must be a sense
of unease   surroundings that are flat
and poorly lit   muffled
                        as if underwater
an apprehension of *déjà vu   déjà*
entendu   an intuition
                                        of edginess in dust

Allow in the idea
                                        of a presence
the horripilation of the unknown   face
at the window   chair that rocks
                        in an empty room
fingers that touch your face in the dark
a thing behind the skirting board
                                        skittering

Overlay the illusion
                                        with shifts of time
time-slips   time-travel   quantum leaps
                        dimensions that reproduce
as if within mirrors   an infinite
repetition of images   smaller
                                        smaller
                                            smaller

Automata on Display, not Moving for Once

Iron-girt, tight as a rivet's grip,
they stand between walls
and barricades.

Someone has taken care
to sculpt the eyes
with a hard gaze.

Once these were inlaid with gems.
Lashes in fine silver
lifted with the dawn. Torsos

shone in muscle and limb as if
nourished by ambrosia and nectar
in the ichor of the gods.

Robotically, they will dismantle
bombs, find survivors in wreckage
or they may overthrow

human constraints, wipe out
systems, abolish structures, free
monsters from caves.

Laboratory Neon

       would suit you, Daedalus,
your personality so phlegmatically cool
and detached.

White-coated in gloves
you could test, sample, meld
human glial cells

with the neurons of a mouse.
A smooth coalescence, and at the end
it's still a mouse.

Neater to work with a brain in a dish
than to carve a frame for a bull
and a queen to copulate in.

How did your minotaur look at its birth?
Tiny and cute in the sweetness of calf
with horn buds under the skin?

What a risk you took. At what stage
did the monster grow out of control?
Next time, work with something

small, easily deniable. Say it's
just a cell, just for science. No animal
will ever be created.

Monologue in a Labyrinth

this is a dangerous place
                        but nothing
                                to be scared of   stop
trembling
monsters are pure myth

a dead end   we're in a mine   the mine's heart
or the dead zone of a tunnel

                                we need to
crawl   this bit
is like a drainpipe   smelly as a sewer
you can wander underground   so they say   if
there's a grating
and people squat down they'll see you

                easy to peer into hades
through a crack in the upper earth

                                can you hear birds
we must be somewhere
near daylight or dusk   this low roof is like a pier
the underside where starlings fly out and there's
seaweed on your face and cold wet sand in your
shoe

            somewhere   there's a way out

On Record Here

If this is a canvas there are women in it, women close to the edge where it's dark. For once they are not over-painted or covered up by a gilded frame.

Athena is first, but she is fickle and unpredictable, as they all were, those goddesses. She has had her day. Let her pass.

Pasiphae, broken, ravaged queen, what is she – a crazy adulteress, a mother who saw her son imprisoned for life and later murdered, or a victim who was as much deluded as the white bull in a green field? He, scenting pheromones in the skin of a dead cow, would have charged at the wooden structure and the woman inside with the mad force of one on full heat. Myth has many versions of rape by bull and they are all brutal.

Ariadne almost manages to reverse the traditional role of princess rescued by the prince. A flash of summer lightning and she is in charge, taking control of events. But her story ends with loss. We leave her, weeping and abandoned, on the shores of Naxos, her hero creeping away with the dawn.

And finally, threadbare at the end of the line, is the slave girl presented as a gift from the ruler to Daedalus. She is mentioned just once in accounts. We are told she gave birth to two sons, one of whom drowned at sea. We can imagine her grief. Her name – let it go on record here – is *Naucrate*.

A Calf for All That

He had a name:
Asterion.
A star-like fruit of love.

Not as his enemies tell it:
a gruesome half and half
rutting in thick bovine skin, a monstrous,
murdering hybrid thing –

See how tenderly he's curling,
cradled on his mother's knee.
An aberration – yes,

but a calf for all that.

Here's a thicket by a cave
where sweet elderberries rot
white-spotted in the mouldy damp
of propaganda's tales.

What if we stand on a different hill,
glimpse the green and spacious meadows
where the girl with lustrous hair,
Ariadne

dances and the morning air
moves with her?

Listen, there's a piper's tune
as Cretan ladies dip and swirl in swift
meander through the maze and feathers
of the curtseying crane
grace the courtship dance.

He had a name, this tiny
deus, offspring of a pure white bull,
too beautiful to kill.

Bearing a Monster and After

She lets her eye wander
from earth to the sky
welcomes the rain on her face
colder than sin.

She knows highs
knows lows, manic
one moment, brittle
cicada the next.

Divorced from touch
(that exquisite sentience)
she is her own landscape
and it's endless.

Ariadne Re-Visits

Statues, in this
room of stone
are solid
in white marble.

Light pales,
a slow afternoon.
The dead
reflect
in windows.

In this green air
a centaur, if not
exactly smiling
loses
its anguished
gaze.

Theseus,
her faithless lover
is armless
and cracked.

More than
content
she slowly
wanders
away.

Athena

Woman, you were incredible:
wise, stupendous, lavish in gold with
ivory flesh –

Athena, once your statue was here
but breath in this space is cold.

What shade
were your eyes?
Which rock is a
shrine, which stone
your puissant heart?

The owl, your familiar, stares
from a tree,
shrewd, single minded,
master
of the strategic pause
and calculated drop.

Lady, you would
appreciate our
dispassionate
control. We need
no birds to track
the sky

for death may be
dealt
bloodless, from a
screen.

Goddess, you have
gifted us
the olive tree. Mine
in the garden
bears no fruit, too
young and small
and far from sun.

This morning its leaves are silver with rain.

Somewhere, beyond my fence, men weep.

An Athenian Mother

They are born to be hostages, our children, hostages
to fortune from the quickening day. Always the joy,
and always the terror of loss.

Often I'd get up at night to check my daughter
breathed, touching her cheek with my finger until
she whimpered in her sleep and stirred.

And many times I called her in from play, too early
and unfairly. But I needed to know she was safe
and under my roof.

We celebrated with a feast the day she left childhood
behind. Green olives, figs, a scatter of herbs and
warm baked bread, wine for the blessing –

wine that soured with the taint of a curse as ten days
later they took her away, left me screaming on the
quayside, and her, trying to be brave

but crying for me as they were led, our young
hostages, onto a ship with a sail of despair, a tall
mast ripping the sky and my heart with it.

Daedalus in the Edgelands

He improvises his steps like a line
from *Bye Bye Blackbird,* or a long loose
thread from a ball of wool. Content
to be lost he turns left, right, strides
to the south; one measure north brings
a feeling for soil, strata, ancient

dances and rain. He is glad to stroll
among the unkempt and dingy, the rubble
the trash and unclaimed, and relieved
for the moment at least, of voices that growl
do this, do that, invent an animation, befuddle
the lusty queen with a wooden cow.

A pause in time, an empty space which is never
really empty, a break from the outer
clamorous world – he thinks of his quiet
hideaway, his den in the cliffs, his haven
where he can study the king's ships without
fuss. The blackbird sings in the tree; one last note.

Exile and the Thread

Exile.
A distance
from home.

Patching up cracks
with putty
scrubbing mouldy
stains of grease
selecting

wallpaper (meadow-
green grasses dotted
with white
marguerites) he
presented

a contented
front.

If inside
during hours and
endless hours
of insomnia

exile
was on his breath

then nobody
guessed.

No redemptive thread
for him

No way out

It was always
deeper in.

Memo:

- Eyeball to eyeball. Finger on lips. Use words with double meanings.

- Find feathers. Long, short, flea-ridden, white-tipped. Any kind. Use your exercise time on the prison lawn to gather a few each day. Guards won't stop you. Too busy watching the port.

- Wait for the message. Be ready. Tell no one not even your sister. You can send for her later.

- Honeybees have built a comb in your cell. Has prison made a dullard of you? Sharpen that inventor's brain of yours. Use yellow wax and a soft thumb.

- The journey will be ferocious. Hour after hour. Cramping. Claustrophobic. No air. Don't panic. Don't panic.

- Find a job for the boy. He's restless and bored confined in a tower. Why is he messing with the wax? Let him sort feathers, order them in size.

- There'll be a beach. A boat. Stand in the water and wait with the rest.

- You need thread. Lots of it. Cut up your shirt if you have to. Teach the boy to tie knots.

- The boat will be too small. Rickety. Perilous. Don't think about it. Don't count heads. Squeeze yourself in.

- Make a start on the arm and shoulder frame. Wings must balance, move in time with currents of air. Trust in your skill, take pride. How safe is the sky? Don't think about it.

- Muffle that cough. If a baby cries, gag it. They'll be watching from every cliff.

- Give clear instructions to the boy. Make sure he listens, takes it all in. What good is your life if you lose him?

- Get ready to jump. Mind rocks. Don't hesitate. Deep breath.

- Two sets of wings. Fasten them with steady fingers. Hold his hand. Go.

The Air is Waiting

He leaves the thickness of darker ground where
words dry up like a chick's
      thin bones

and feels his own bones lifting as he slips out of
gravity and soars
      wherever the winds allow

and understands at last the workings of wing and
muscle, the quill's uplift
      the meaning of sky.

This is his vision. When there's trouble in winter
men think about flight or
      in imagination

seek alternatives. Yet flight is not for the timorous.
Wings that are feathered
      scorn and reject

the middle way, risk sea salt and the sun's heat
and are in the domain of birds, gods
      and the seraphim.

Lost in Flight

A silhouette mid-fall, an endless rhyme
again and again, obsessive refrain –
the cloud and the mud, the dove and the slime.

A single image in memory's chain
soldered with silver, is riveted, linked
again and again, obsessive refrain.

W*hat if, what if* – why do you think
dawn will show in a cold grey sky? Starlight's
soldered with silver, riveted, linked

in a circle, a ring – and he is lost in flight
above the salt sea, below the white sun.
Dawn is showing in cold grey sky. Starlight

is quenched. A new refrain, *he is gone, gone* –
This is his elegy; let him go, over,
above the salt sea, below the white sun.

Image, circle, memory's chain; below is
a silhouette mid-fall, an endless rhyme.
This is his elegy. Let him go. Over
the cloud and the mud, the dove and the slime.

For Those Who Are Falling

for you are falling wingless from a high tree
into the space between air

and the soil

which is nothing but space

a headlong drop

to plummet through in darkness
and be hurt by

unless

you find yourself caught on a branch
budding and green

which holds you as if with a prayer
for the coiling and binding of leaves or twigs of
grace

while above you a small bird rises
with a song cool as raindrops

unparching your earth and offering such stillness

you do not need to fall into the dark
wingless and hurt

The Black Sail 2

They say he carved a detailed, intricate design
on Apollo's temple doors. A frieze in gold

a storyboard about two cities, signs
and omens, riddles, lust, the uncontrolled

outcomes of the single thread, the monster's
slaying, the blunder of the ship's black sail

that proclaimed *the hero is slaughtered* –
and that was it, the reminder, the nail

in his skull, the fall, the drowning, his son
dead – Icarus his son, dead.

No way could he show it, praise the sun
whose heat was ice, whose golden light bred

death of a child, his child. Wretched.
The worst. Meaning of leaving. The end.